THE GOSPEL FOR KIDS

by Kathryn Slattery

Illustrated by Frances and Richard Hook

Chariot Books™
David C. Cook Publishing Co

For my children

Chariot Books™ is an imprint of David C. Cook Publishing Co.
David C. Cook Publishing Co., Elgin, Illinois 60120
David C. Cook Publishing Co., Weston, Ontario

THE GOSPEL FOR KIDS
©1989 by Kathryn Slattery for text and David C. Cook Publishing Co.
for illustrations

Book and cover design by Ron Kadrmas
Hook art on pages 6 and 23 used by permission from Tyndale House
Publishers, Inc.

First Printing, 1989
Printed in Singapore
94 93 92 91 90   5 4 3 2

Library of Congress Cataloging-in-Publication Data

Slattery, Kathryn.
   The gospel for kids / Kathryn Slattery; illustrated by Frances and
Richard Hook.
       p.   cm.
   Summary: A retelling of the Gospel, emphasizing how Jesus can be
your friend and Savior.
   ISBN 1-55513-992-2
   1. Jesus Christ—Juvenile literature. 2. Bible stories. English—N.T.
Gospels [1. Jesus Christ. 2 Bible Stories—N.T.] I. Hook, Frances, ill, II.
Hook, Richard, ill. III. Bible, N.T. Gospels IV. Title.
BT302.S553 1989
232—dc20
                                                            89-7143
                                                              CIP
                                                              AC

A Note to Grown-Ups

As the mother of two small children I am reminded daily that young people do, indeed, possess a very active inner life and can be surprisingly curious about religious and spiritual matters.

Consider just a few of my five-year-old daughter Katy's questions about Jesus, God, faith, death, and heaven:

- "When Jesus was born, was it before or after the dinosaurs?"
- "If God is invisible, how can we know He is real?"
- "How can God and Jesus be the same?"
- "But my friend Peter says he doesn't believe in God."
- "Mommy, what happens to me after I die?"
- "Up in heaven, does Grandpa know it's my birthday?"

I've also been surprised to observe that even at the tender age of five, my daughter is already being exposed to the darker sides of human nature. Even within her seemingly sheltered worlds of home and family, school and friends, she grapples daily with complex and sometimes painful feelings of rejection, temptation, peer pressure, guilt, anger, and anxiety:

- "Emily says she isn't my friend anymore!"
- "Megan says it's OK to say, 'shut up.' How come you and Daddy tell me it's wrong?"
- "I know I'm not supposed to talk in the library, but when I sit next to Sarah, it's so hard not to."
- "Sometimes, Mommy, I love my teacher more than you. I hope that doesn't make you too sad."
- "But what if when it's my turn, I feel too shy to sit on Santa's lap?"

I was nineteen years old—a bewildered and unformed college sophomore in the turbulent late sixties—before I ever heard the Gospel presented in a clear, easy-to-grasp, meaningful way. To this day it is that moment—the night I first heard the Gospel and asked Jesus Christ to come live in my heart—that remains the single most important, life-transforming, and personally helpful event in my life.

Too bad, I've often thought, that so many years had to pass before I first heard the Gospel and believed. Even as a small child—especially as a child—might not I have benefited from the priceless gift of a personal friendship with Jesus?

It is in direct response to questions like those posed by my daughter that I have written this Gospel for children. And because it is for children, I have emphasized the unique nature of Jesus as the ultimate Friend.

It is this, after all, that I think every person, at every age, yearns for. . . .

A friend.

A real friend.

A friend who is faithful. A friend who is all forgiving. A friend you can trust. A friend whose presence makes you feel deep down good inside. A friend who will laugh with you and cry with you. A friend to whom you can call out anytime, anywhere, and know He will be there. . . .

This is the Friend I've come to know and love in Jesus Christ. This is the Friend Jesus I want my children and—through this book—children everywhere, to come to know and love as well.

Kathryn Slattery, New York City

Long, long ago . . . ever so many years after the dinosaurs, and almost two thousand years before TV . . . a baby boy was born in the tiny town of Bethlehem in the tiny country of Israel.

We know this is true.

It is an historical fact.

But because it happened so many years ago, long before there were things like telephone directories and computers, we don't know for sure the exact day this baby boy was born. Or the exact address.

We do know that He was born in a stable, which is like a small barn.

He was born in a stable because hospitals hadn't been invented yet, and because there was no room at any of Bethlehem's inns for the baby's family, who was visiting from out of town.

The baby's mother was named Mary. Her husband was a man named Joseph. But many months earlier, before Mary even knew she was going to have a baby, a beautiful angel named Gabriel had visited her to share with her this great mystery: "You are going to bear a son," Gabriel told Mary. "And His true Father will be God in heaven."

As Gabriel had instructed, Mary named her baby Jesus, which means *Savior*, or "One who saves the people."

And to this day, He remains the most important person who ever lived in the history of our world.

Why is Jesus so important?

Because of who He is, and because of the extraordinary things He said and did during His life here on earth.

What are some of the things Jesus said and did?

Well, for starters, Jesus said He was God's very own Son—and everybody knows how important God is!

Jesus was so close to God that when He prayed, or talked to God, He used the word "Abba," which in Jesus' Hebrew language means "Daddy," or "Papa."

Jesus said that God, His Father in heaven, had sent Him to planet earth to bring people love and forgiveness and peace and happiness. He said that His Father God had sent Him to show people everywhere once and for all what God was really like.

*U*ntil Jesus was born, you see, no one had ever seen God.

No one was sure what God was really like.

Was God grouchy? Was He friendly? Was He funny? Was He sad? Did God even care much about us at all? Or was He just too busy doing important things like keeping the stars up in the sky and the planets from bumping into each other?

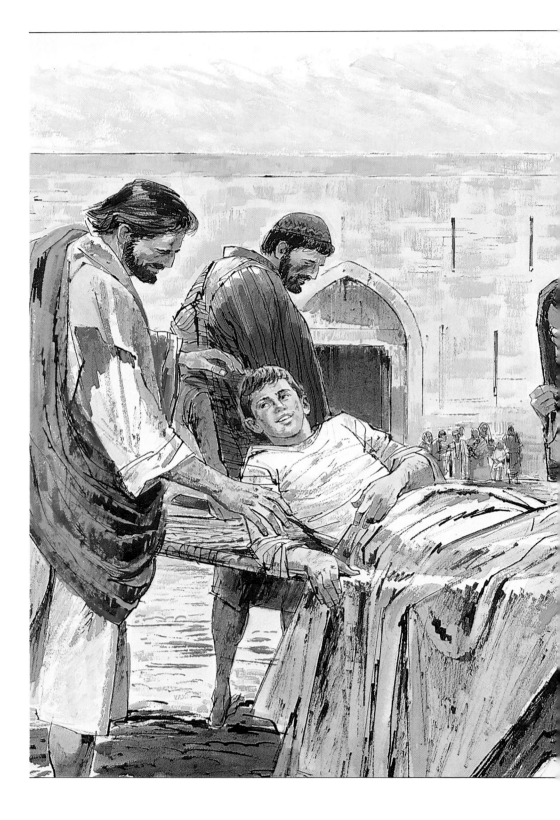

*J*esus said that God cared about each and every one of us—you and me—A LOT.

"Listen to what I say and watch what I do. I will show you what My Father God is like, and how much He cares about you," said Jesus.

To show the people what God is like, Jesus did a lot of loving, kind-hearted things like make sick people well, and blind people see, and deaf people hear.

When people were sad, He cried with them. When people were happy, He laughed with them. He was a good friend.

Jesus did all these things to show how much God loves and cares for us. Jesus did all these things so that people everywhere —including you and me—would believe that He really truly was God's Son—and so that we would believe in God, too.

There is another very important thing about Jesus.

And that is that He loved children.

Though Jesus never got married and had any children of His own, He deeply loved all the boys and girls He met. And the children loved Him back.

Grown-ups, Jesus said, could learn a lot from children.

Children, He explained, were experts when it came to believing in God.

"Let all the little children come to Me and believe in Me and in My Father God," Jesus said. "And as for you grown-ups, you try and be a little more like children this way yourselves, understand?"

*M*any of the grown-ups understood what Jesus was trying to teach them, and loved Him.

But others didn't.

And, when Jesus was still a young man—just 33 years old—He died. He was killed by unhappy, fearful people who didn't like the things He said and did. These were people who just couldn't find it in their hearts to believe in Jesus. These were people who had forgotten how to be like children in their hearts.

Now, since Jesus was God's Son, He could have stopped these people from killing Him. But He didn't. By choosing to die, He took the punishment for all the bad things people do and think. Jesus died to save everyone on earth who would believe in Him. That's why He is called our Savior.

*H*ow sad people were on the day Jesus died!

His mother and brothers and sisters and friends—all of them missed Him terribly. They cried and cried.

If only Jesus could somehow come back and be with us, they thought.

But that was impossible. Never again would they hear the sound of Jesus' laughter, listen to His stories, feel His big bear hugs.

They took His broken, lifeless body and laid it gently in a tomb, which was like a small dark room carved into the side of a grassy hill. They rolled a big rock over the opening to the tomb and then—their hearts nearly breaking with sorrow—they all walked away.

*T*hree days after Jesus died, early in the morning, Jesus' friend, a woman named Mary Magdalene, set off to visit the tomb. But when she arrived, the big rock had been rolled away. The tomb was empty. Her beloved Jesus was gone!

It was soon after that Mary made the most extraordinary, wonderful, important discovery. . . .

Jesus was ALIVE!

The tomb was empty because Jesus — in the most mysterious, awesome, miraculous way — was no longer dead, *but had come back to LIFE!*

*H*ow happy everyone was to see and be with Jesus again!

Once again He talked and laughed with His mother, brothers, and sisters. He even had a picnic on the beach with some of His best friends. Once again they all gathered around Him and listened to His stories.

Jesus said that soon He would be going back to heaven to live with His Father God. But before He left, He had some very good news.

Everyone listened carefully.

The good news," said Jesus, "is that because I have come back to life, you too can live forever with Me and My Father in heaven. My Father loves you so much, He wants this for you. He wants you to believe in Him and Me. He wants to forgive you for all the wrong things you do. He wants you to live with Him forever."

Jesus explained to His family and friends that because they loved and believed Him, after their life on earth ended they would find themselves alive in heaven with God and Him.

It would be such a happy time!

Like a big birthday party.

Everyone in heaven is happy and healthy. There is no more sadness or crying or pain.

"In heaven," said Jesus, "God will wipe away every tear from every eye."

*T*here is one last thing Jesus told His family and friends before He returned to heaven to live with God.

He told them that although He could no longer stay with them in person, there was a very special way He could stay with them in their hearts.

"I will send you My Holy Spirit," said Jesus. "He will live in your hearts, and teach you, and guide you, and comfort you—just the way I've been able to do while I've been with you here on earth."

And that is exactly what Jesus did.

Even today, right now, Jesus can be alive in our hearts through His Holy Spirit.

Even today, it is possible to listen to His voice . . . hear His laughter . . . practically feel His hugs.

More than anything, right now, Jesus wants to live in your heart.

He wants to be your friend.

The kind of friend who will help you know right from wrong. The kind of friend who will forgive you even when you make mistakes, and love you no matter what. The kind of friend who will make you feel deep down good inside.

Jesus wants to be the kind of friend you can talk to when you're sad, when you're happy, when you're in trouble—anytime at all!

Yes, Jesus wants to be your Savior and friend—the best you ever had.

*I*f you're not sure Jesus is living in your heart already, would you like to ask Him in?

It's easy.

Just talk to Him like this:

"Hi, Jesus! I just want to let You know that I believe in You and in Your Father God. Thank You for forgiving me when I'm wrong, and for loving me the way You do. Please come into my heart now and live in me and be my friend. I love You, Jesus. And I'm really excited about being Your friend, too."

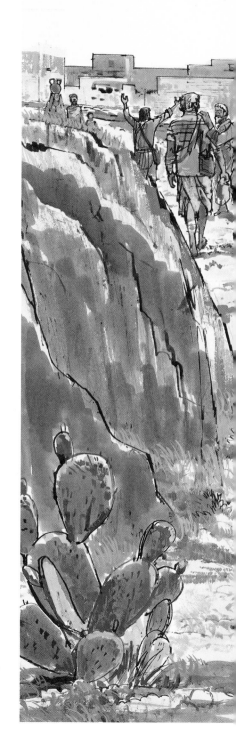

Once you've prayed this prayer (for that's what prayer really is— talking to Jesus!) you will be beginning a new adventure in your life unlike any other.

Wherever you go, whatever you do, Jesus will be with you, living in your heart, helping you in all kinds of ways.

Whenever you want Him, just say, "Hi, Jesus!" And He will be with you—listening, caring, being the best friend you ever had.

Now that you've reached the end of this book, you're about to begin a brand new story.

A true story.

A story that begins here and now. In your heart.

It is the story of your new life and the special friendship that's yours forever with Jesus.